DANGEROUS MAMMALS

WOLVES

Madison Parker

Norwood House Press

Library of Congress Cataloging-in-Publication Data:

Names: Parker, Madison.
Title: Wolves / Madison Parker.
Description: Buffalo, NY : Norwood House Press, 2025. | Series: Dangerous mammals | Includes glossary and index.
Identifiers: ISBN 9781684502714 (pbk.) | ISBN 9781684502721 (library bound) | ISBN 9781684502738 (ebook)
Subjects: LCSH: Wolves--Juvenile literature.
Classification: LCC QL737.C22 P375 2025 | DDC 599.773--dc23

Published in 2025 by
Norwood House Press
2544 Clinton Street
Buffalo, NY 14224

Designer: Ocean Books
Editor: Kim Thompson

Photo credits: Cover, p. 1 Volodymyr Burdiak/Shutterstock.com; p. 5 Holly Kuchera/Shutterstock.com; p. 6 MiloWeller/Shutterstock.com; p. 7 Grindstone Media Group/Shutterstock.com; p. 9 Chase D'animulls/Shutterstock.com; p. 10 Giedrilus/Shutterstock.com; p. 11 RealityImages/Shutterstock.com; p. 12 Mi Paithanker/Shutterstock.com; p. 13 John L. Absher/Shutterstock.com; p. 15 Michal Martinez/Shutterstock.com; p. 16 PNQ Images/Shutterstock.com; p. 17 JiVa Images/Shutterstock.com; p. 19 Ghost Bear/Shutterstock.com; p. 21 AB Photographie/Shutterstock.com

Printed in the United States of America

CPSIA compliance information: Batch #CW25NHP: For further information contact Norwood House Press at 1-800-237-9932.

TABLE OF CONTENTS

Meet the Wolf 4
Types of Wolves 6
Favorite Foods 14
Staying Safe Around Wolves 18
Glossary 22
Thinking Questions 23
Index 24
About the Author 24

MEET THE WOLF

A wolf is a wild animal that looks like a dog. Wolves are **mammals**. Baby wolves drink their mother's milk.

TYPES OF WOLVES

Gray wolves are large and have thick fur. They live in forests and mountains in North America, Europe, and Asia. They can be dangerous when defending their **territory**.

Arctic wolves live in Earth's Arctic Circle. Their white fur blends in with the snow. They can be dangerous when they are protecting their babies.

Red wolves are small. They live in the southeastern United States. They are shy, but they can be dangerous when they feel **threatened**.

Ethiopian wolves are skinny and have red and white fur. They live in Ethiopia’s mountains. They avoid people, but they can be **aggressive** when they are scared.

Indian wolves are small and have **tawny** fur. They live in India's grasslands and forests. They sometimes attack animals on farms.

Himalayan wolves have thick, pale fur. They live in the Himalayan Mountains. They are **elusive**, but come out to protect their territory.

Mexican wolves are the smallest wolves in North America. They will fight to protect their homes.

FAVORITE FOODS

Wolves are **predators**. They hunt in packs. Wolf packs work together to catch big animals like deer and elk.

Wolves also eat smaller animals like rabbits, birds, and fish. They eat whatever food they can find.

Sometimes, wolves eat fruits and vegetables. They like berries and apples. These foods give them extra **nutrients**.

STAYING SAFE AROUND WOLVES

If you see a wolf, stay calm. Do not run. Running might make the wolf chase you. Keep looking at the wolf as you slowly move away.

Never feed a wolf or get close to it. Stay a safe distance away.

If a wolf seems aggressive, shout loudly. Try to make your body look big by standing tall and raising your arms. This might make the wolf go away.

GLOSSARY

aggressive (uh-GRES-iv): threatening; ready to attack

elusive (i-LOO-siv): very hard to find or capture; shy

mammals (MAM-uhlz): animals that are warm-blooded, that have hair or fur, that usually give birth to live babies, and that produce milk to feed their babies

nutrients (NOO-tree-uhntz): substances such as protein, vitamins, and minerals that are needed by living things to stay strong and healthy

predators (PRED-uh-turz): animals that live by hunting other animals for food

tawny (TAW-nee): having a light, sandy-brown color

territory (TER-i-tor-ee): an area that is occupied and defended by an animal and that often contains the animal's nest, den, or home

threatened (THRE-tuhnd): in danger of being harmed

THINKING QUESTIONS

1. Why are wolves mammals?
2. What kinds of food do wolves like to eat?
3. What should you do if you see a wolf?
4. How are the Arctic wolf and the Mexican wolf alike and different?
5. Where do wolves live?

INDEX

baby/babies 4, 7

farms 11

forests 6, 11

fur 6, 7, 10–12

grasslands 11

mountains 6, 10, 12

North America 6, 13

packs 14

ABOUT THE AUTHOR

Madison Parker spent her childhood in the city of Chicago, Illinois. A farm girl at heart, today she lives in Wisconsin with her husband and four children on a small farm with cows, goats, chickens, and two miniature horses named Harley and David. Her favorite dessert is vanilla frozen custard with rainbow sprinkles, even in the winter.